W9-BEH-996

Flag Day

By Margie O'Hern

Scott Foresman
is an imprint of

Glenview, Illinois • Boston, Massachusetts • Chandler, Arizona •
Upper Saddle River, New Jersey

Photographs

Every effort has been made to secure permission and provide appropriate credit for photographic material. The publisher deeply regrets any omission and pledges to correct errors called to its attention in subsequent editions.

Unless otherwise acknowledged, all photographs are the property of Pearson Education, Inc.

Photo locators denoted as follows: Top (T), Center (C), Bottom (B), Left (L), Right (R), Background (Bkgd)

CVR © 2007 Thomas Eimermacher/©California Academy of Sciences, David Stoecklein/ Corbis, © Richard Levine/Alamy Images; **1** Martin Plomer/©DK Images; **3** © isifa Image Service s.r.o./Alamy Images; **4** © DK Images; **5** Martin Plomer/©DK Images; **6** © Richard Levine/Alamy Images; **7** © Richard Levine/Alamy Images; **8** ©Stockbyte/SuperStock

ISBN 13: 978-0-328-46358-9
ISBN 10:   0-328-46358-2

Copyright © by Pearson Education, Inc., or its affiliates. All rights reserved. Printed in the United States of America. This publication is protected by copyright, and permission should be obtained from the publisher prior to any prohibited reproduction, storage in a retrieval system, or transmission in any form or by any means, electronic, mechanical, photocopying, recording, or likewise. For information regarding permissions, write to Pearson Curriculum Rights & Permissions, One Lake Street, Upper Saddle River, New Jersey 07458.

Pearson® is a trademark, in the U.S. and/or in other countries, of Pearson plc or its affiliates.
Scott Foresman® is a trademark, in the U.S. and/or in other countries, of Pearson Education, Inc., or its affiliates.

8 9 10 V010 14 13

We have a special flag.
We call it the American flag.

Our flag has 50 stars.
The stars are white.

Our flag has 13 stripes.
The stripes are red and white.

Our flag has a special day.
That day is June 14.
We call it Flag Day.

We honor our flag.
We sing songs and wave
small flags.

Our flag is important to us.
It stands for our country.